Kangaroo Island
South Australia

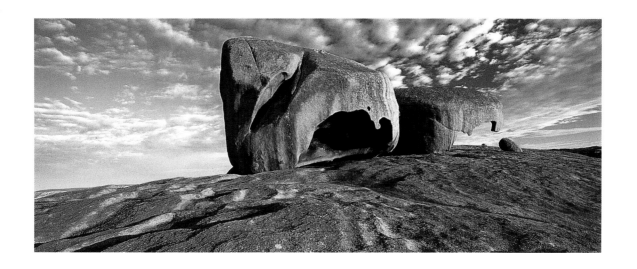

Text by Cil Dobré
Photography Pete Dobré

National Library of Australia Cataloguing-in-Publication Data:
Dobré, Cil.
Kangaroo Island South Australia
ISBN 0 9577063 4 0
1. Kangaroo Island (S. Aust.) - Pictorial works.
I. Dobré, Pete, 1958- . II. Title.
919.4235

Published and distributed by Pete Dobré's Oz Scapes
P.O. Box 305, Happy Valley, South Australia, 5159, Australia
Email: ozscapes@cobweb.com.au   Phone/Fax: +61 8 8381 5895
Website: www.petedobre.com.au

Photographs copyright © 2001 by Pete Dobré
Text copyright © 2001 by Cil Dobré
Printed in Hong Kong

Front Cover: Remarkable Rocks
Title Page: Remarkable Rocks

Behind every act of creation lies the Creator.

THE
BUREAU Pre-Press
Specialists

FUJIFILM
Professional

TJM
PRODUCTS

Nikon

Atkins·Technicolour

BRIDGESTONE

Map of Kangaroo Island

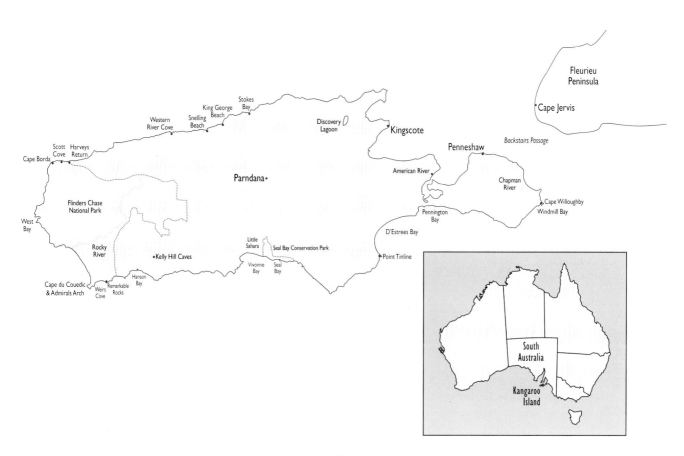

Stokes Bay

King George Beach

Western River Cove

Snelling Beach

Discovery Lagoon

Kingscote

Penneshaw

Backstairs Passage

Fleurieu Peninsula

Cape Jervis

Scott Cove

Harveys Return

Cape Borda

American River

Chapman River

Cape Willoughby

Windmill Bay

Parndana

Flinders Chase National Park

West Bay

Rocky River

Pennington Bay

D'Estrees Bay

Kelly Hill Caves

Little Sahara

Seal Bay Conservation Park

Point Tinline

Vivonne Bay

Seal Bay

Cape du Couedic & Admirals Arch

Weirs Cove

Remarkable Rocks

Hanson Bay

South Australia

Kangaroo Island

Kangaroo Island

Full of natural beauty and amazing wildlife, Kangaroo Island (K.I.) is unique.

While this third largest island off Australia's coast (155 kilometres long and up to 55 kilometres wide) may appear small, it has amazing diversity in attractions and wildlife. Plan adequate time to enjoy a special part of South Australia.

K.I. lies 30 minutes from Adelaide by air, or 15 kilometres by ferry across Backstairs Passage.

Aboriginal people once lived on K.I., but early in 1802, when British explorer Matthew Flinders made the first European sighting of the island, it was uninhabited. Flinders came ashore. The crew feasted eagerly on fresh meat, hence the name 'Kanguroo Island.' (The spelling changed later.)

After one month Flinders left, and soon after a French corvette 'Le Geographe' arrived. On a rock a sailor carved 'Expedition of discovery by Commander Baudin aboard the Geographe 1803.' A replica of the carving, known as Frenchmans Rock, at Penneshaw is protected by a white dome. Baudin returned in the summer of 1802/03 to map much of the south and west coastlines, hence the many French names.

In the early 1800's white people came to live. Sealers, escaped convicts and runaway sailors who lived on kangaroo and wildlife, traded salt, seal, kangaroo and wallaby skins for tobacco and spirits.

The Duke of York arrived in July 1836 with official settlers, to establish the first free settlement in Australia. However, insufficient water and suitable building timber hindered them. After 4 years the site was abandoned, favouring Adelaide.

The late 1800's saw the pastoral industry established. Grains were grown. Timber, kangaroo, possum and wallaby skins and eucalyptus oil were sold. After WW2 ex-soldiers farmed the undeveloped land on the island's central plateau.

With isolation, drought and dropping rural prices, many islanders turned to tourism. B&B's, local crafts, gourmet food, tours, unique island products like eucalyptus oil and K.I. wines initiated an important industry - tourism.

Wherever you drive, walk, sail or fly, K.I. colours shine out. The ocean is deep, vivid blue. White spray crashes into aqua bays. The sunsets reflect on rugged, golden cliffs. Winding country roads are surrounded by iridescent green rolling hills in winter or golden brown fields in summer. Appreciate the blue, purple, pink, yellow and red wildflowers in Spring, together with diverse flora.

K.I. contains National Park, Conservation Park and Wilderness Protection Areas, with undisturbed bushland. Stroll and view koalas with their young at close range, as they chew eucalyptus leaves. See echidnas by the road, digging for a meal of ants, while a sand goanna basks in the sun. Visit K.I.'s famous Flinders Chase - a sanctuary for native Australian animals. Walk amongst the smaller, dark K.I. long furred kangaroos, and observe the waddling Cape Barren Geese.

Drive cautiously on island roads in the fading evening light when tammar wallabies line the roadside.

Home to a large colony of rare Australian Sea Lions, Seal Bay is exciting. Seals bask in the sun, frolic in the shallow waters or catch a wave in the Aquatic Reserve.

For birdwatchers, K.I. is a paradise. Birds live on coastal cliffs, estuaries, creek and river systems, lagoons and wetlands, in the mallee and heath. Visit little penguin colonies. Hear their chatter through the night. Watch wedge-tailed eagles soaring, waiting to descend and devour roadside kill. See osprey ride the thermals in search of prey. Marvel as a white-bellied sea-eagle hovers above you. Graceful pelicans and glossy black-cockatoos live at various locations on the island. Enjoy the stunning colour of the male superb fairy-wren.

Come to K.I. to fish. With jetties located in picturesque bays and long sandy beaches, you can throw out a line. Charter a deep-sea boat, fish off rocks, or cast into the surf. Rivers like the Chapman River are popular for a catch.

When visiting K.I's white lighthouses, discover the history and isolation of the mid - 1800's. Mainland S.A. depends on these lighthouses for weather reports.

K.I. boasts a worldwide reputation for locally produced gourmet foods. Savour the honey of the Ligurian bee, Camembert, Brie, Haloumi and Yoghurt made from the milk of island sheep, the succulence of corn-fed chickens and K.I. wines. Taste varieties of fish, oysters, lobsters and marron.

Numerous attractions provide memories. Enjoy the beautiful stalactites, stalagmites and twisted helectite formations in the large underground system at Kelly Hill Caves. Climb a wind-swept dune at Little Sahara. Enjoy the rugged, isolated north coast.

Discover roaring surf and deserted beaches. Wind through the rock tunnel at Stokes Bay. Watch the sun glow on the orange rocks at Windmill Bay and King George Beach. Marvel as waves crash at Admirals Arch at sunset. See the NZ Fur Seals bask at Cape du Couedic rocks. Awesome Remarkable Rocks with precariously-balanced boulders on a smooth granite dome is our special K.I. location.

A day visit only skims the surface of this wonderful island with so much to enjoy. Whether you sail, fly, drive, join a 4WD or bus trip, favour yourself and come for at least a week. You will wonder and contemplate the beauty of creation.

North Coastline - Winter

North Coastline - Winter

West Bay - Flinders Chase National Park

West Bay - Flinders Chase National Park

Hanson Bay

Vivonne Bay

Koala

Tammar Wallaby

Kangaroo Island Kangaroo

Echidna

Brushtail Possum

Little Sahara

16

Discovery Lagoon

17

Chapman River

Kelly Hill Caves

Kelly Hill Caves

Kelly Hill Caves

Kelly Hill Caves

New Zealand Fur Seals

Cape du Couedic Lighthouse

Cape Borda Lighthouse

Cape Willoughby Lighthouse

Seal Bay Conservation Park

Seal Bay Conservation Park

Seal Bay Conservation Park

Seal Bay Conservation Park

Seal Bay Conservation Park

Seal Bay Conservation Park

Cape Borda

Cape du Couedic - Flinders Chase National Park

Scott Cove

North Coast

Approaching Snelling Beach

Snelling Beach

Western River Cove - Winter

Western River Cove - Summer

Little Penguins

Pelican

Rosenberg's Sand Goanna

Pelican

Rocky River - Flinders Chase National Park

Rocky River - Flinders Chase National Park

Stokes Bay

46

Frenchmans Rock - Penneshaw

Penneshaw - Winter

48

Kingscote

49

Rugged Coast Near Windmill Bay

King George Beach

Pennington Bay

Pennington Bay

Western River Cove

Harveys Return

Point Tinline

Admirals Arch - Flinders Chase National Park

Kangaroo Island Kangaroo

Cape Barren Geese

Superb Fairy-wren

Boxing Kangaroo Island Kangaroos

Weirs Cove - Flinders Chase National Park

Flinders Chase National Park

Remarkable Rocks - Flinders Chase National Park

Remarkable Rocks – Flinders Chase National Park

Sunrise – Penneshaw